MICHIGAN STORIES FOR NEWCOMERS

Senem's Journey to a New Beginning

Barbara Vaille and
Jennifer QuinnWilliams

Illustrations by Barbara Goodsitt

THE UNIVERSITY OF MICHIGAN PRESS
Ann Arbor

ISBN 0-472-03145-7
(978-0-472-03145-0)
Published in the United States of America
The University of Michigan Press
Manufactured in the United States of America
⊗ Printed on acid-free paper

2009 2008 2007 2006 4 3 2 1

To the Reader:

This book was written for your pleasure. It is written in simple English for adult English language learners. We hope you will enjoy the story and learn English at the same time. When a character is speaking in Turkish, the speech appears in *italics*. When a character is speaking in English, the type does not change. Senem's English is not always perfect, of course, but it is written for authenticity of someone at her language level.

Happy Reading,
Barbara and Jennifer

Dedicated to Ruhane, Oguz, Senem, and Erdem

CHAPTER 1

Senem and Tarkan were in their car, driving to a party. The radio in the car played classical music, and the night was warm but not too hot. Their four-year-old son, Hasan, was with the babysitter, Emine.

Senem was worried about something.

"Tarkan," she said, *"Emine was acting strangely this afternoon."*

"What did she do?" he asked.

"Well, you know, she's returning to Turkey in a few days. She started to cry really hard because she said she is going to miss Hasan so much!"

Tarkan looked quickly at his wife, then back at the road. *"Maybe it's because when she gets to Turkey, her little nephew who she loved so much won't be there. Maybe Hasan reminds her of her nephew."*

"Yes, I think you're right. It was just strange."

They arrived at the party. They got out of the car and walked to the front door. Tarkan said, *"When we get home, we can talk to her and try to help her feel better."*

Senem smiled. *"That's a good idea. Now, let's enjoy the party."*

The sounds of laughter and quiet music were all around Senem and Tarkan as they walked into the living room. There were a lot of people at the party. There were pretty women talking to men who were smiling. People from all over the world were talking with each other. Some people were from their country, Turkey. Some people were American, and others were Mexican or Dutch. Everyone seemed to be having fun. Soon, both Tarkan and Senem were talking and laughing with friends. After a couple of hours, Senem looked around for Tarkan. He was on the other side of the room. He was talking to their friend, Ruth, and her husband, Dan. Senem wondered if Tarkan was telling them about his classes at the University of Colorado at Denver and his master's degree. Then Tarkan and Senem and their son, Hasan, would return to their home in Ankara, Turkey.

Senem wanted Tarkan to look over at her. It was getting late, and she was tired. She wanted to go home. Finally, he looked at her, and she pointed at her watch. He nodded. He said something to Ruth and came over to her side.

"Are you ready to go home?" he asked in Turkish.

"Yes. I'm starting to get a headache from so much English."

"You're doing so much better, though. Remember last year? You didn't even want to go to parties."

Senem laughed. *"Yes, but I can cheat at this*

party. I can speak Turkish to lots of the people here. But I also told Emine we would be home by 10:00."

"She won't mind if we're a little late," said Tarkan.

"No, but she baby-sat for me this afternoon, and she is baby-sitting for me again tomorrow. I think she needs a little break."

Tarkan and Senem found the host of the party. They thanked her and walked through the party to the front door. It took a long time because along the way they had to stop and say goodbye to friends. Finally, they walked out into the warm June night. As they drove home, Tarkan said, *"That was fun, wasn't it? You met some new people, and all our friends were there."*

"Oh, yes, I had a good time. But, sometimes I still feel like a puppet with strings attached to my head, mouth, and jaw. My head moves up and down by itself. I don't say anything."

"Just guess what they're saying. You'll probably get it a little right. You know, we only have one more year in the U.S.A."

"I know!" said Senem. *"Emine and I were talking about it earlier today. That's when she started to cry."*

"I'm not really thinking about Emine right now," said Tarkan.

"Oh, really?" laughed Senem. *"Pardon me. What are you thinking about?"*

"Well, I'm thinking about you, and having another baby," said Tarkan.

Senem turned her head quickly to look at him. A baby. She didn't know if she wanted another child. Here in the United States, she didn't always have much to do. Sometimes she was bored. But in Turkey she was very busy. She was a bookkeeper for the government. She didn't know if she could raise two children and work.

"Now is the perfect time for us," said Tarkan. *"If you get pregnant now, the baby will be born before we return to Ankara. You can rest and relax all the time. If we wait until we get back, you'll have to work so hard, the pregnancy will be much more difficult."*

"But, Tarkan, I don't know if I want two children."

Tarkan was silent. Then, he said, *"I do."*

Neither of them knew what to say after that. Finally, Senem said, *"I'll think about it. You think about it, too, and we'll talk tomorrow."*

Tarkan nodded as he pulled the car into the parking lot next to their apartment building.

"Are you mad?" asked Senem.

"No. Are you?"

"No, of course not. I need time to think."

Tarkan nodded again. As they walked into the building, he put his arm around Senem. It was dark inside except for one or two lights down the hall. Just before they got to their door, Tarkan stopped. He looked at his wife with a smile. *"If I pull your string, Miss Puppet, can I get a kiss?"*

"We're in public," Senem said, but she giggled and turned her face to his.

He pulled her close. They shared a long kiss. Then Senem pulled away. *"Let's tell Emine we're home."*

Tarkan used his key to open the front door. The apartment was quiet and dark. The computer screen glowed from the corner of the living room.

"Hello, Emine, we're home!"

No one answered. Senem looked in the kitchen while Tarkan checked the bedrooms. They met in the living room. Senem had a feeling of panic in her stomach. They looked at each other. Where were Emine and Hasan?

"I'll go see if her car is outside," said Tarkan. At that moment, the telephone rang. Senem answered it. *"Hello?"*

"Hello, Senem. This is Emine."

Senem smiled and made an Okay gesture at Tarkan. He looked relieved. *"Yes, Emine, where are you?"*

"Alex came over, and we decided to take Hasan out for a while."

"To the park? At this time of night?"

"Oh, just out. Hasan is having a great time."

"That's fine, but please come back now. It's getting late."

"Don't worry at all," said Emine.

"Emine, it's past Hasan's bedtime. My English class starts tomorrow, and he has pre-school. I think you should come home now."

There was a pause. Then Hasan's voice came

over the line. *"Mama, we're playing trip! We're driving in the car to special places! We had ice cream, and we're going swimming when we get to the hotel!"*

Senem laughed, nervously. *"Staying in a hotel? That's quite a trip! I hope you'll be home soon."*

Another pause. Then Emine again. *"So, as I said, don't worry about us."*

"Emine, I don't understand what's going on."

Tarkan was getting more and more upset as Senem talked. He asked Senem to give him the phone. She frowned and shook her head. He put his face next to hers and shouted, *"Emine? Where are you? What do you think you're doing? Come back immediately! Bring Hasan home!"*

Then Emine said, *"Just don't worry about us. We'll probably be back later. Goodbye, Senem."* She hung up.

Senem stood by the phone. There was something strange about that "goodbye." Emine never said when they would be home. It was unusual for Alex, Emine's boyfriend, to be with them. He worked nights. Where were they? Driving somewhere? Why didn't Emine say when they would be home?

"Did she hang up?" shouted Tarkan.

"Alex is with them so they are okay."

"How do you know? Call her back. Tell them to come home."

Senem dialed Emine's cell phone number.

There was no answer. She dialed Emine's home phone number. Emine's message came on the line. She turned to Tarkan. He looked frightened and worried and angry. He looked like she felt.

"Call Alex," said Tarkan.

"I don't know his number. I don't even know his last name. Oh, Tarkan, what should we do? Should we go and look for them?"

"Where? They could be anywhere."

"Hasan said they had ice cream and that they're going to a hotel. Should we drive to hotels and look for the car in the parking lots?"

"Senem, that's crazy. There are hundreds of hotels around here." Tarkan sat down on the sofa. *"Let's think. This is very strange. Why won't she tell us where they are going or when they'll be back?"*

Senem sat next to Tarkan. Her voice shook. *"Remember when I said Emine cried this afternoon because she has to go back to Turkey next week?"*

"Tell me more about what happened," said Tarkan.

Senem told Tarkan about what happened when Emine came over that afternoon.

"It was hot in the apartment," Senem explained. *"Even with two fans turned on high, it was hot."* She recalled every detail and told Tarkan how she looked at the sky out the living room window. There were dark clouds everywhere, just like yesterday and the day before. The rain started falling lightly at first. Senem closed the window. The clouds turned

darker and began to move in closer all around. Suddenly lightning flashed across the sky and thunder boomed. Senem yelled a little in surprise. Thunderstorms scared her. She wanted to hide, but she heard Hasan cry out from the bedroom.

Tarkan stopped Senem. *"Was Hasan scared?"*

"Only a little," said Senem. *"He wondered what the loud noise was. He asked why it was dark outside."*

"What did you say?"

Senem said, *"I told him it was raining. I took him into the living room with me to cuddle up on the couch to watch the storm through the window."*

Hasan asked, *"Mommy, why is the rain white? It's hitting the window."*

Small, round pieces of ice tapped the window pane.

"That's not rain. That's hail. Oooh. How sad. It's tearing the leaves off the trees."

Then, almost as quickly as it began, the hail stopped. The ground beneath the window was covered with green leaves. A thin layer of hail on the leaves looked like snow. It was still raining, but not as much. The clouds started to break up and move toward the east. The sun came out and made the water on the wet leaves look like diamonds. Senem pointed at the sky at a beautiful rainbow that arced over the city.

"*Look—a rainbow!*" Senem said to Hasan. *"Let's go outside and get some hail. We can put it in the freezer and show Daddy. And we can see if the mail came at the same time."*

Hand in hand they went outside. The air was cool now. They gathered some of the pea-sized hail and quickly formed two freezing balls.

"My fingers are cold," laughed Hasan.

Back in the apartment, Hasan sat on Senem's lap. She opened a children's book and described the different pictures in a low voice. After a few minutes Senem looked down at her son. He was asleep. Senem smiled. He was so cute with his curly dark hair, big brown eyes, and long eyelashes. He looked just like his father did when he was a boy.

Carefully, Senem moved Hasan to the couch next to her. She heard a knock at the door. Emine came in, and Senem kissed her on the cheek.

"The storm woke Hasan up," she said. *"He just went back to sleep."*

Emine nodded and went over to look at Hasan. When she turned around, Senem was surprised to see tears in Emine's eyes.

"I will miss Hasan so much," said Emine.

"Don't worry," said Senem. *"You'll see him again. We'll be back in Ankara in only one year."*

"Yes," said Emine. She was really crying. She gulped as she said, *"But he won't remember me. He's only three years old. One year is a lifetime for him."*

Senem didn't know what to do. She and Tarkan both liked Emine very much. They first met her at the university where Tarkan was studying. She helped them many times by baby-sitting. In return, she used Tarkan's computer to do her university homework when he wasn't home. Senem didn't expect her to be so heart-broken about leaving Hasan. But she remembered that Emine's nephew in Turkey moved to Germany with his parents. Maybe Emine was just realizing that she wouldn't have either of the boys she loved near her.

Senem was shaking as she told the story. She stopped for a minute. Tarkan put his arms around her, and she told Tarkan what she said to Ermine.

"Emine, you can spend lots of time with Hasan until you leave. And when you go, we'll put a photograph of you in Hasan's room. We'll tell him stories about you and show him the picture. He won't forget you. Next year, when we see you again, he'll think of you as a favorite aunt." Senem patted Emine's hand. *"Don't worry!"*

Emine gulped again. She dried her eyes. *"I must be tired,"* she said. *"I'm working so hard. I still have one paper to finish before I go. I'm spending a lot of time with Alex, too. He doesn't want me to leave. He even asked me to marry him. But I'm not ready. I've been working so hard to get my degree, and now I must get a job."*

Senem and Emine talked about Alex and what Emine should do. Senem advised her not to see him until her paper was done. "*You can work on it some more right now while Hasan takes his afternoon nap,"* said Senem. *"After you hand it in, we can talk more about Alex."*

"Thank you. You are like a sister to me," said Emine, with tears in her eyes again.

Senem smiled. *"I'll be back from the art museum at about 4:00. You can have dinner with us, and then Tarkan and I will go to the party. You'll have the whole evening with Hasan."*

❖

Senem said to Tarkan, *"That's everything that happened this afternoon, and now Emine and Hasan are gone."* Senem took Tarkan's hand. *"I'm afraid Emine has done a foolish, stupid thing,"* she said. She tried not to cry, but tears poured down her cheeks. *"I think she took Hasan because she doesn't want to leave him behind when she goes back to Turkey."*

Tarkan squeezed Senem's fingers. *"They can't get far,"* he said. *"They don't have his passport."*

Suddenly they both looked at each other and raced into the bedroom. Tarkan pulled a suitcase out of the closet. The lock on the suitcase was broken. He threw the suitcase open. He grabbed the envelope where he kept their passports. He turned it upside down and shook it. Two passports tumbled out. Hasan's passport was gone.

CHAPTER 2

Senem let out a little cry. Tarkan took her into his arms. They stood for several moments, not talking and barely breathing. Finally Senem said, *"Let's call Ruth. She will know what to do."*

Her fingers shook as she dialed their friend's phone number.

"Hello, Ruth? Is Senem. We have very big problem. Emine and Alex take Hasan. Do we call police?"

"WHAT? You mean they're gone? Emine and her boyfriend kidnapped Hasan? How do you know?" Ruth sounded confused.

"Talk to Tarkan," Senem answered. She gave him the receiver.

"Hello, Ruth," Tarkan said. "They were not here when we came back from the party. Then telephone rang. It is Emine. She said they are out. Hasan talked. He said they are going to a hotel. Emine said they come back later. We don't know when is 'later.' And they took Hasan's passport."

Ruth said, "You stay there. I'm coming over. Jeremy is in bed, so Dan will stay here. This is serious. We need to call the police."

They both hung up the phone. *"Ruth said we have to call the police,"* said Tarkan.

"We have to call the police? What do we do? Do we call 911? Shouldn't we wait until we hear from Emine again? Maybe 'later' means later tonight."

Soon the doorbell rang. Ruth rushed in and hugged them both.

"Oh, my gosh. I can't believe it!" she said. "Okay. Tell me everything from start to finish." They both told Ruth what happened in English.

"This is terrible!" said Ruth. "First we need to call the police."

"Are you sure?" asked Senem. "Emine will not hurt Hasan. She love him."

"Yes, but they took him. And we don't know anything about Alex. We don't know how long they'll keep him or where they plan to go. But they took his passport, so I think you have to think of the worst-case scenario."

"Excuse me? I don't understand," said Senem.

"We have to think about the worst thing that could happen and go from there. Something's wrong with Emine. She's not thinking right. She probably wouldn't let Alex hurt Hasan, but you never know. Maybe they are just taking him for the evening. But maybe they are going to try to take him to Turkey."

Tarkan said, "We thought that also. Senem said Emine was sad and crying today about leaving Hasan. She is going back to Turkey in a few days.

She is afraid he will not remember her. He is like her nephew who moved to Germany."

"But he is my son!" cried Semen. "Where is he?"

"First we call the police," said Ruth. "Do you want me to call for you?"

"Maybe is best," said Tarkan. "Senem and I are not in good condition to speak on the telephone in English."

Ruth dialed 911. "Hello. This is an emergency. I want to report a missing child. I am calling for my friends who are from Turkey."

Senem and Tarkan sat close together as they listened to Ruth answer the questions of the police dispatcher. After a few minutes, Ruth hung up the phone. "A police officer is coming over right away," she said. "There's something called an Amber Alert. It gets the word out to the public about a missing child. I don't know anymore about it. While we're waiting, let's look it up on the Internet and see what it says."

"Okay," said Tarkan.

Senem and Ruth looked over Tarkan's shoulders as he searched for Amber Alert on the Internet. Ruth put her arm around Senem's slender, tense shoulders.

"Scroll down, Tarkan," said Ruth. "Those first few entries are stories. There, click on that, the one that shows the Amber Alert plans for all the states in the U.S. Now, go to the one for Colorado. Let's read what that says."

The three of them stared intently at the screen. They read the Colorado Amber Alert Plan.

"Look at the Criteria section," said Ruth. "It says the child must be in immediate danger of serious bodily harm or death. What do you think?"

"No!" Senem said immediately. "Emine will not hurt Hasan. She will not let Alex hurt him also. Maybe she is not think clearly, but she will not do this. I am sure."

"Let's keep looking. Tarkan, click on Missing Children. Let's see what that says."

"You look," said Senem. "I can't watch computer anymore."

They discovered a lot of interesting information, including parent support groups and all the agencies that can help in recovering a lost child.

A few minutes later they heard the doorbell. There were two police officers at the door. One was a man wearing a neatly pressed uniform. A badge on his chest said Denver Police Department. The other was a woman who was not dressed like a police officer.

"Hello. My name is Officer Watson, with the Denver Police Department. This is Detective Sanchez from the Missing Persons Bureau. We got a call about a missing child. May we come in and ask you a few questions?"

"Yes, of course," said Tarkan. "Please come in and sit down." He was always polite. Senem wanted

to scream, *"Help us get our child back!"* But she knew Tarkan's way was better.

When they were all seated, Officer Watson got out a form and began to ask routine questions. He asked them their names, address, and phone number. He asked for Hasan's passport number. Then he asked when they had last seen Hasan. "Who was he with?"

Tarkan answered, "Emine Bahar and her boyfriend, Alex. We don't know his last name."

The officer wrote that down and asked what they thought Emine and Alex would do and what had happened so far. Tarkan told the story again. He said they didn't think Emine and Alex would hurt Hasan.

"What is your son wearing?" Detective Sanchez asked.

Senem answered, "He wears blue short and red shirt with white lines. Oh, I didn't think. Maybe he has jacket. I will look." Senem went into Hasan's room. When she came back a moment later, she was pale and had tears in her eyes.

"His new backpack is not there. He is so excited to have it, like the big kids. And I look in his drawers. Some shirts and pants are not there."

Ruth put her arm around Senem. "Come sit down," she said gently.

"I'm sorry ma'am. Could you give me a description of the clothing and backpack? The more detailed information we have, the better it is for our search. The first few hours are the most important."

Senem and Tarkan described everything they could think of.

"What happens now?" asked Ruth.

Officer Watson responded, "I'll file this report and get the information out to all the officers on duty. If anyone sees them or has any other information, they will report back to the police station. Then we'll contact you."

Detective Sanchez handed Tarkan her card. "Call me immediately at this number if you get another phone call or remember anything else that might help us in our investigation. My department will be in charge of the investigation."

"Emine is friend. I know she will not hurt our son. Maybe they return tonight," said Senem.

"I hope so, ma'am. But call us right away if they do. Keep the man and Miss Bahar here until we arrive. Even if your son is unharmed, they kidnapped him, which is a felony. They are already in trouble with the law."

"Oh, no!" cried Senem.

Tarkan's eyes were dry. He did not have any sympathy for Emine or Alex. "Senem, they took our son! I hope they put them in jail!"

"Oh, Tarkan..."

The officers moved toward the door. "We'll leave you folks now. Try to rest. If we have any news, we'll be in touch with you right away."

Ruth said, "When we looked up Amber Alert on the Internet, we read that we should call 911 and other law enforcement agencies like the sheriff and highway patrol. And also call radio and TV stations. What do you think?"

"Yes, that's a good idea," answered Officer Watson. "We'll be following up on everything I put in my report. Let me give you the case number. Other agencies can access the report through the police department, but they may want to get their own information from you, too. It would be a good idea to stay by the phone for the next day or two."

After the police officer left, the three sat in silence. Finally Ruth said, "Let's make those calls."

For the next 20 minutes, Ruth helped find the numbers and called several radio and TV stations. She gave out the case number and gave them a description of Hasan. When she was finished, she said, "I'm going home. But call me if anything happens. Call any time, day or night. Try the house or my cell phone. Jeremy has preschool. I'll come over after I drop him off."

"Oh, school!" said Senem. "I forgot. Summer session starts tomorrow. Hasan wanted to see his friends. He look forward to this. And I will miss my English class, too."

"Don't you worry about that, Senem. They'll be happy to see you no matter when you start. I'm thinking good thoughts about Emine bringing Hasan back soon! I'll see you tomorrow."

"Goodbye, Ruth. Thank you for helping us. You are a real friend," said Tarkan.

"You bet. I'm glad I could help."

❖

It was a long, sleepless night for Senem and Tarkan, but there were no telephone calls. Tarkan had just started summer vacation, so he didn't need to worry about missing classes. Senem phoned her friend, Martha, and told her what happened. The two women always walked to English class together. Martha would have to go alone today. Martha promised to call Senem after class.

A little before 10 AM, the phone rang. It was Detective Sanchez calling to see if Senem had heard from Emine. As soon as they hung up the phone, it rang again. Tarkan answered.

"Daddy, we are having an adventure! Emine took me swimming last night, and we are going again today."

"Hasan, I am so happy you called. Are you okay? Can I talk to Emine?"

"Yes, Daddy. We are having fun." Tarkan heard him give the phone to Emine.

"Emine, where are you? We called the police. They are already looking for you. You must..." Tarkan heard a click as Emine hung up the phone.

CHAPTER 3

The next day was fuzzy in Senem's mind. Her memory of the call from Detective Sanchez was vague. Ruth stopped by with dinner. Martha called. Senem felt like she was moving in slow motion.

Tarkan and Senem called their families in Turkey. They said that the baby-sitter and her boyfriend took Hasan. Both families were surprised and upset. Senem's mother wondered how a true friend could do such a thing. Finally, it was time for Senem to go to bed.

The next morning, after sleeping soundly, Senem woke up slowly. She felt strange. Something was making her feel very sad. She turned to find Tarkan. He was not in bed with her. Then she remembered everything. Hasan. Quickly, she got out of bed. She put on her robe, and she walked into the kitchen. Tarkan was sitting at the table with a steaming cup of coffee in his hands. He was staring into the cup as though it might tell him where Hasan was.

"Tarkan?" asked Senem.

Tarkan looked up. *"I didn't sleep well."*

"I wrote a journal entry for my English class," said Senem. She pushed her journal across the table to Tarkan. *"Will you read it?"*

Tarkan shook his head. *"Please, not right now."*

Senem's eyes filled with tears. If she were in Turkey, all her sisters and their husbands and her parents would be with her night and day. Here, in the United States, she had to rely on Tarkan. But, he was as sad and helpless as she was. Senem wanted to be where there were many loving, caring people.

"I changed my mind. I think I will go to English class this morning," she said. *"Is that all right? I want to be around people."*

Tarkan nodded. He rubbed his eyes with his hand. *"I'm so tired. I will stay here and try to sleep and listen for the telephone."* Senem put her hand on his shoulder. He reached for it and kissed it.

"I'll take the cell phone," Senem said. *"Call me if you hear anything."*

She got dressed, had a cup of coffee, and left for school. It was too late to meet Martha now, so she went alone. As she walked, she thought about the class. Last year, when she and her family were new to the United States, she joined an English class at a local public school. She enjoyed it very much. The teacher, Karen, became her good friend. She met women and a few men from all over the world. When she was lonely or sad, her new friends in the class helped her. She needed their help now.

She knew she had made a mistake as soon as she entered the class. There were so many new students. She had forgotten that yesterday was the first day of the summer class. Yes, there were many faces she knew, but there were more new faces. Cute, noisy children were everywhere. Hasan would love seeing so many new children. Hasan. Suddenly, Senem felt dizzy. Her face turned white, and she reached for a chair to sit down.

Karen and Martha rushed to her side. Karen put her arms around her. "Senem, it is so good to see you," she said. "Martha told me what happened. How are you doing?"

Martha said, "I surprise to see you."

Senem's throat felt tight. She couldn't speak. She handed her journal to Karen.

"Is all here," she whispered. "I'm sorry. I can't stay."

Karen looked worried. "Do you want me to call Tarkan or Ruth to give you a ride home?"

Senem nodded. "Please. Call Ruth. Tarkan needs to be near phone. And, will you read my journal?"

Karen nodded, took the journal, and called Ruth. Then she asked Martha to help the students get organized while she read Senem's journal.

Senem's Journal, Tuesday, June 15

I feel you are my true friend. I can tell you anything. I hope is OK that I write how I am feeling now. In Turkey we say I can not press the pain to my heart. It means I must tell you. I think you understand. I sit here in apartment, with no life in. Hasan does not bother me. He does not say to me turn on TV, or to play game with him. Is he happy? Is he crying? Emine loves him, but she is not his mother. She does not know all to do for him. Can she take him away for all time? Can she be so cruel? She hurts me, Tarkan, and even Hasan. Tarkan is very angry. He wants to hurt Emine. I am sad most of all. Emine is almost like a young sister. But Tarkan and I both want same thing. We want Hasan. Now, I cannot tell you more English. I know you understand.

Karen closed the journal. She put her arm around Senem and looked into her eyes. "I'm not going to write back today," she said. "Thank you for trusting me with your feelings. I would like to bring dinner over for you and Tarkan tonight. May I?"

Senem nodded. While Karen turned her attention to the class, Martha walked outside with Senem to wait for Ruth.

"I coming to your house after class," Martha

said. "I bringing food. Carmen and Flor coming too. We wait with you."

Senem smiled, once again unable to speak. She nodded.

❖

When she and Ruth got home, Tarkan was in bed, but the living room was not empty. Two friends from Tarkan's master's program were there. Senem and Ruth made tea, and soon Martha, Carmen, and Flor arrived. They brought enchiladas and rice and beans. More friends came in the afternoon. The apartment was full when the phone rang. Everyone stopped talking and eating.

Senem picked up the phone. Tarkan came hurrying from the bedroom.

"Hello?" Senem tried to sound confident and strong.

Emine answered. Her voice was shaky. *"Senem. I know what I am doing is wrong."*

Senem was careful in her answer. *"Yes, Emine, you are right. You must come home now."*

"But you must hate me," whispered Emine. She was crying. *"I only wanted to keep Hasan with me. I can't go back to Turkey without him."*

"Yes, you can," said Senem. *"Remember what I told you? We'll put your picture in his room, you'll see him in Turkey in only one short year—"*

"No, no, you'll never let me see him. I've done a

terrible thing. That's why I have to take him with me now. I'm so sorry, Senem. I have to take him. Alex says you'll never let me be with him again."

Senem gasped. *"Emine, that's not true! Alex doesn't know me. I don't hate you! I just want to have Hasan back with me, his mother, and with Tarkan. A child needs his parents. Think of that, Emine, a boy without a mother or father."*

"An orphan," cried Emine. *"That's an orphan. He's not an orphan. He has me and Alex."*

Tarkan was standing by Senem's side, breathing heavily. His face was red with anger. Ruth was holding his arm, as if to keep him back from the phone. Senem looked at him. With her eyes, she tried to tell him to be quiet. She put her finger to her mouth.

"Without us, he is an orphan," she said, softly. *"He needs us, his mother and father. He needs you, too, but he really needs us very much."*

"He cried today," Emine admitted. *"He cried for you and for his daddy. He cried until he fell asleep, and he still looks sad. I don't want him to be unhappy. Senem, I don't know what to do."*

"Bring him home to us, please, please," begged Senem.

In a small voice, Emine said, *"Come downstairs. Come alone. You can see him. You can kiss him goodbye."*

Senem couldn't stop a small shriek of surprise and pain. *"Goodbye? Kiss him goodbye?"*

Tarkan understood immediately what was happening. With a roar, he ran to the door. With Senem behind him, he flew down the stairs and out the apartment building. But Emine and Alex were leaving. Senem and Tarkan could see Alex at the steering wheel. The tires of the car screeched as it pulled away quickly. Alex ran the stop sign, and they were gone.

Senem and Tarkan stood in the street. Tarkan bellowed, "HASAN." Senem began to cry. Friends held them and led them back up to the apartment. They sat close together. Ruth called the police.

"He was right here, and we didn't even get to see him," Senem said. *"Right downstairs all the time we were talking."*

"We didn't know," said Tarkan.

The police arrived quickly. They assured Tarkan and Senem that it would be only a matter of time now before Emine and Alex were caught.

"Now we know they're in Denver," Officer Watson explained. "They can't get far. We have her license number and a description of the car. I bet we get them within the hour."

"Emine is very upset," said Tarkan. "She might do something crazy."

"More crazy than steal our child, come to our house so that we can say goodbye to him, and then steal him again?" Senem screamed. *"What's more crazy than that?!"* She realized she had spoken in Turkish. It seemed like everyone understood what

she meant, even if they didn't understand the words.

Martha handed Tarkan a cup of tea. "Give some tea," she said. "Senem, she need the tea."

Senem sipped the tea gratefully. She felt like the real world was slipping away. She watched the police officers leave. She watched her friends and Tarkan's classmates talk and make more tea. She felt like a character in a scary folktale. She was the mother whose child is stolen by goblins or witches or a monster. And all she could do was sit, sit some more, and wait.

In the middle of this nightmare, she heard a quiet knock at the door. All of their friends seemed to be watching her. She was unable to move. Tarkan walked across the room and opened the door.

Emine stood in the doorway. Her long black hair was messy around her face. Tears poured down her round cheeks. In her arms, she held the sleeping Hasan.

CHAPTER 4

Senem took Hasan from Emine, trying not to wake Hasan up. She held him close, rocked him in her arms, and kissed the top of his head. She wept. Tarkan came to her side and hugged them both. Then he led them to the couch.

The air in the room suddenly seemed very tense. Then, almost like clockwork, Martha motioned Flor and Carmen to go into the kitchen with her. Everyone knew what to do. Tarkan's two friends went to stand by the door. Ruth quietly slipped into the bedroom to call 911. Tarkan looked up from watching his wife and son.

"Emine," he said in a low voice, shaking his head slowly from side to side.

Emine crumpled. She slid to the floor and sat there, curled up in a ball. Her face had a scared look, as if she were a caged animal. Her eyes were wide with fear. Tarkan almost felt sorry for her. But when he glanced at Hasan, he remembered in an instant all the worry and panic of the last 48 hours, and he had no pity.

A police siren grew louder as it came racing through the streets. It stopped outside their apartment building.

Detective Sanchez and Officer Watson rushed in to the apartment. Detective Sanchez knelt by Emine while Officer Watson asked Tarkan questions. Ruth moved to be near Senem and to help Tarkan with his testimony. The police had the report of the 911 call from Ruth. They checked the accuracy and added Tarkan's information.

"We have officers looking for the car with the male suspect. We'll need to take Miss Bahar into custody. Does she have any family here who can come with her?" asked Officer Watson.

"No," answered Tarkan. "She was here studying for two years and is going back to Turkey. She already has a reservation and ticket for two days from now."

"Is there anyone you know who can assist her? I don't think she can manage alone." They looked over at Emine. She was now sitting in a chair, wrapped in a blanket. Detective Sanchez was trying to get her to talk, but she still had the lost, faraway look on her face. "She's in shock. I've just called for an ambulance. She'll need to go to Denver Health until she comes out of this. But someone should go with her. Do you know anyone who can help us out?"

Tarkan looked toward the door at his friends. One of them said, "We will go. She is our friend also. And we both come from Turkey, but not same city."

"Thank you. We appreciate this," said Detective Sanchez.

At that moment the paramedics arrived and quickly checked Emine's condition. Then they met with the police officers and put Emine gently on the stretcher, and tucked the blanket around her. Detective Sanchez asked one of the friends to ride in the ambulance with Emine and the other to drive to Denver Health and meet them at the emergency entrance. Then she turned to Tarkan and Senem.

"We won't be able to get a statement from her until tomorrow. She'll be in a secured area at the hospital for the night. The paramedics would like to check your son for any signs of abuse or shock," said Detective Sanchez.

Senem was surprised. "But he is fine. He is resting. He is tired."

"I understand, Ma'am. But we must. It won't take long," answered one of the paramedics. "We'll be gentle." He quickly checked Hasan's arms, legs, stomach, back, and neck for bruises. Then he shined a flashlight into Hasan's eyes to see if the pupils were too big. Hasan cried and held on to his mother.

"He looks fine. If you notice anything strange on his body or about his behavior, bring him in to the emergency room at Denver Health. You don't need an appointment."

Detective Sanchez prepared to leave. She said, "Unless Officer Watson has some more questions for you, we'll be going now. Someone in the department will be in touch with you in the morning."

Officer Watson said, "I'm finished for now. I know you are anxious about what will happen to Miss Bahar. We'll have more information tomorrow. We'll contact you when we've found Miss Bahar's car and her boyfriend. I'm sincerely happy that you have your son back safe and sound."

Tarkan and Senem thanked the officers, paramedics, and their friends, and took one last look at Emine as they all left. Tarkan closed the door and then sank into a chair.

"What a day!" said Ruth. "I'm going home now and let you have some alone time and get some rest. I'll check in tomorrow. Maybe you'll know something by then. If you need me, you know where to find me."

Just then Martha came out of the kitchen, followed by Flor and Carmen. They had washed the dishes and put the food away.

"We go home now, too. Don't worry for dinner tomorrow. We called Karen. She will bring food."

There were tears in Senem's eyes again. She was still sitting on the sofa holding Hasan. He was sleeping again.

"Thank you very much. You are all good friends to me. I am lucky."

When the others left, Senem said, *"Tarkan, I can't leave Hasan alone by himself in his room tonight. I'm going to sleep with him."*

"Bring him in to our bed, Senem. Let's be together."

Hasan was so tired that he never really woke up. The last few days had taken a toll on him, too. Although the bed was crowded, it was comforting.

❖

The next morning, the clock on the bedside table said 9:25 AM. Tarkan got up and opened the curtains. The sun was shining, and the sky was blue.

"Wake up, you sleepyheads. It's a beautiful day. It's a good omen. Let's call Turkey. We need to tell our families the wonderful news. But first, my son, let me give you a big hug." Tarkan went back to bed and opened his arms. Hasan rolled over until he was engulfed in his father's embrace. *"Daddy!"* he said. Senem watched them with a smile on her face and in her eyes.

It was already early evening in Ankara. Not everyone was home in either Senem's or Tarkan's family. But they were able to talk to Senem's mother and her sister and Tarkan's mother. They were all very relieved.

"Oh, I have been worrying about you so much! And my mind made up stories that kept me awake. That's one less thing to bother me," said Senem's mother.

"What do you mean, Mama? What do you have to worry about? All your children are safe and happy now."

"Well . . ."

"Well what? Tell me."

"It is nothing for you to bother about."

"Mama. Tell me."

"It is just some earth tremors. There were a few small ones west of the city, and in towns almost as far as the coast. I hope it isn't getting ready for a big one."

"You worry too much," Senem said.

The call to Tarkan's mother was similar. They both were overjoyed by the news of Hasan's return, and they both talked about the tremors.

"We will have to watch the news to see if anything comes of this," Tarkan said to Senem.

❖

Around 11:30 Detective Sanchez called and reported that Emine slept off and on during the night. The nurses said she didn't answer them when they asked her if she felt any aches or pains or if she was thirsty. They assumed that she didn't speak English. The two friends had been a great help. They went home shortly after midnight and promised to go in to help in the morning. They were able to get Emine's keys so the police could check her apartment. The detective hadn't gotten those reports yet.

"Since your son has returned safely, our department doesn't have power in this case. People at the federal level will take over now because Miss

Bahar is a foreign visitor here. She has broken the law and will likely have to go to court. In that case, she would have a court-appointed attorney represent her. Then it would be up to the judge if she is deported or fined. The biggest problem right now is that she doesn't answer our questions. This afternoon, she'll be checked out by the staff psychiatrist."

"This is very complicated now," said Tarkan. "So many different officers and doctors. And the young man, Alex. Did you find him?"

"Yes, he was arrested very early this morning at his apartment. He says this whole thing was his idea."

Tarkan sighed. "Why did he do it?"

"He says he just wanted Emine to marry him. Somehow, he thought an act like this would show her how much he loved her," said the detective.

Senem interrupted. *"Tarkan, ask the detective if we can visit Emine."* The look on Tarkan's face told Senem that he was still very angry with Emine, but he asked the detective the question.

"It's not a good idea. In fact, the court could see that as interfering. It would be better not to do anything for a couple of days. We'll have a better picture of what's going to happen then."

Senem felt very sad for Emine. When Ruth stopped by a while later, Senem said, "Is so sad. Emine did wrong thing, but she is good person. She is very smart and always get high scores on her papers and tests. She had good future in Turkey. Now, I don't know. Maybe all chances are ruined. I think this Alex, he fooled her. He makes her think this is good idea. But Hasan is safe home now. That is most important to me. I feel strange—angry and sad for Emine at the same time."

"I don't know what I'd do if anything happened to Jeremy," said Ruth. "It is too bad about Emine. But, you know, at least she came to her senses. At least she brought Hasan back."

Hasan was sitting quietly beside Senem. She stroked his hair. The TV was on, and he was staring at the screen. He was still not himself.

Senem looked at Ruth and then at Hasan. Ruth understood that Senem was afraid to talk about Emine and the incident in front of her son even though he was not paying attention to them. The two women went into the kitchen. Hasan didn't look up.

"I think I understand why Emine took Hasan. When she lived in Turkey she liked very much her nephew. He moved to Germany. I think suddenly she understood—no Hasan, no nephew. No little boy!" said Senem.

"Really? I had no idea," said Ruth. "She seemed so happy most of the time."

"I am very scared about Emine," said Senem. "If she get deported to Turkey, it will be bad for her. I think Turkish court will not be easy with her. Maybe she will go to jail or worse."

"Worse? What do you mean?" asked Ruth.

"I don't know. In Turkey we have expression 'eye with eye; tooth with tooth.' "

"Yes, 'An eye for an eye; a tooth for a tooth.' What do you mean?" asked Ruth. "Do you think they would banish her from her family?"

"No, not that. But I don't know what the criminal law say is punishment for this crime."

CHAPTER 5

Senem had nightmares, night after night. In the nightmares, Hasan was always walking away from her with a strange man. She couldn't yell, couldn't scream, and couldn't move to grab him. He slowly walked farther and farther away. He never looked back. She usually woke up scared and sad.

She began to check on Hasan in his bed several times each night. Often, she brought him into her bed. Tarkan complained, but Senem wanted him near her. She held his hand tightly whenever they left the apartment. She made him sit in the shopping cart when she was at the grocery store. She followed Hasan around the playground when he and Jeremy played. One day Ruth said, "Senem, you're acting like a mother hen. You can see Hasan from this bench. I'm tired of chasing the boys around like guard dogs! Sit down."

"Oh, you are right," said Senem. "You are right."

But Hasan felt his mother's fear, and he did not let her sit for long. "Mama, we're going to the slide. Come on." He would not go to the other side of the playground without her.

Ruth was always honest. "Watch out, you're creating a monster," she warned. "What will happen if you ever have another baby?"

Senem agreed, but she didn't tell Ruth that she and Tarkan were having arguments over whether to have another baby. She wasn't sure that she wanted another one. She only wanted to keep Hasan safe in this big, dangerous place.

Ruth saw that Senem looked uncomfortable with her question. She changed the subject. "What's the word on Emine?"

"I'm sorry, I don't understand," said Senem.

"What's the situation? Has she been deported?"

"Oh, yes, last week. The government say, said, she made a felony. A person from another country facing criminal charge can be deported. The judge said because she didn't hurt Hasan or do bad things to him, Emine needed to go back Turkey . . . back to Turkey."

"How did Tarkan feel about that?"

"So angry. He is so angry about everything."

Ruth nodded. "I guess he feels betrayed."

"Yes. And I feel so, too. Now, Emine is in jail in Turkey. She will have a trial. Is that right, trial?"

"Yeah, with a judge and jury and all that."

"Is a little different in Turkey. But we have court system. I think Emine will be treat fair."

"Really? You were so worried about it before. You don't think she'll be mistreated?"

Senem smiled. "I contacted her mother. Her

mother engaged very good woman lawyer. Now, I don't worry too much about her. But don't tell Tarkan! He doesn't want me to help."

"You really are a wonderful person, Senem. Not too many mothers could be so forgiving."

"I forgive, but I can't forget. I think I understand Emine," said Senem. "She had much pressure to do well in school, all things building up at once, get ready to leave U.S. and go back to Turkey, find job in Turkey. Also, Alex wanted to get married. And she wasn't sure about that. Very difficult time. She made big mistake because of difficult time, and Alex made big mistake, terrible mistake."

"We'd say she was 'stressed out,' and Alex took advantage of it."

"Exactly," said Senem. "And I prefer to remember Emine as she was most of time. Friendly, funny, good person. She was good to me, good to Hasan. I can't think too bad things about her."

"What about Alex? What's happening with him? Have you heard anything?" asked Ruth.

"He is in jail. He told police it was his fault. He said Emine was under his influence. Is that right? Influence?"

"Yes. Do you know when his trial will be?"

"No, but it is soon."

The women sat and watched their children play. It was a sunny, hot summer day. They were glad that the bench they sat on was under a big, shady tree.

"Will you have to testify?" asked Ruth.

"I think maybe no," said Senem. "Alex says he is guilty."

"Will Emine have to come back here for the trial?"

"No. She told court her story, and then she was sent back. Also, I think because Alex takes the blame, she doesn't have to be here."

Before they left the park, Senem put her hand on Ruth's arm. "Ruth, I say again I forgive Emine, but I don't forget. She was like sister, and she took my child. Now she's far away. I don't worry about her. I worry about all other people."

Ruth nodded. "I see," she said.

That evening, Tarkan wanted to talk about having another child again. They were sitting in the living room, listening to music, and sipping tea.

"This is a good time for the pregnancy," he said. *"When we go back to Turkey, you will be too busy. We'll be trying to find a house and then moving in. And you will be working again. You should get pregnant now while you have lots of free time and can rest all day."*

"Rest?" asked Senem. *"Do you think all I do all day is rest? I take care of Hasan and play with him. If I don't want to play, he says, 'I want Daddy. He will play with me!'"*

Tarkan laughed. Senem smiled, but she continued, *"I have to shop and cook and clean and try to make our life comfortable here in America. I'm taking*

English class and learning how to drive. Do you think that just because I don't have a paying job that all I do is rest?"

"Of course not. I know you do a lot. I just think it would be easier for you to be pregnant here. That's all. Sometimes you say you're bored."

"Tarkan, how can I keep two children safe? I only have time to care for Hasan and keep him safe."

Tarkan sighed. *"Sometimes I curse Emine and Alex. They stole our peace. Are they going to stop us from having a baby?"* Senem put her arms around Tarkan. They held each other tight.

"What if Hasan had disappeared forever?" whispered Tarkan. *"We need another child. If something bad happens to one, we will have the other one to love and to comfort us."*

"Yes," said Senem. *"You are right."* She pulled away from him. She held his face in her hands. *"But I still need more time."*

Tarkan sighed again. *"I can wait a little longer. We'll still be here for another year."*

Senem nodded. She got up and went into the kitchen to do the dishes. Her muscles felt tight from the stress of the last few weeks. Her head ached. The warm, soapy water helped her relax. As she washed and dried each dish, she felt better. This was something she could control. Clean dishes. A tidy kitchen. If only she could feel this way about the rest of her life.

❖

The next day, Senem drove Ruth's car slowly through an empty parking lot. It was her fourth driving lesson. Jeremy and Hasan were at preschool. Senem carefully shifted from first gear to second gear.

"Great!" shouted Ruth.

The car stopped.

"Sorry!" said Senem and Ruth at the same time.

"I startled you," said Ruth. "Try again."

"Ruth, you are kind. I think I never can learn to drive."

"You are learning! Practice makes perfect. Try again."

Senem put the car in neutral and turned the key. She shifted into first gear and started off again. This time, she shifted easily into second and Ruth directed her to leave the parking lot. They drove on a quiet, residential street. They rolled the car windows down because it was a beautiful day.

As they drove, Ruth talked. She told Senem to shift gears, put on her brakes, or stop at a stop sign. Ruth told Senem about her childhood, but Senem didn't listen carefully. She was focused on driving.

Then Ruth asked, "Why do Muslim women cover up?"

Senem explained that God wanted women to be modest and to help men resist temptation.

"Do you believe that?" asked Ruth.

"Yes," said Senem. "But I think Allah will forgive me for not wearing the veil."

"So, do you think you should?"

"God wants me to, but He will forgive me. I live a clean life." She glanced over at Ruth.

"Wow," said Ruth. "That's interesting—you're a little close to the curb, Senem—I like that idea—oh, watch out, turn a little. . . . Hey!"

Senem drove the car right up over the curb. She drove onto someone's lawn and stopped. The bumper was almost touching a decorative light pole.

"Whoa!" laughed Ruth. "You're supposed to stay on the street!"

"I hurt car? Sorry, very sorry!" Senem didn't think it was nearly as funny as Ruth seemed to.

"Hey, Senem, calm down. No harm done. Everyone makes mistakes learning to drive. Looks like no one's even home. Let's just back up, nice and slow."

"Back up?"

"Shift into reverse."

"Reverse?"

"Go that way." Ruth pointed behind them.

"Oh, yes, I remember. Reverse."

Senem looked at the stick shift. Reverse, reverse. How did reverse work? She pushed in the clutch and shifted the gear, and the car lurched forward. It bumped into the light pole with a thump and died.

"That was fifth gear," said Ruth. Her voice sounded like she was trying not to laugh again. "Reverse is next to fifth."

"I kill car," said Senem. The more she tried to get the car out of this spot, the worse her English became.

"Not likely," said Ruth. "Come on, try again."

"But, the light. Maybe it will be damaged."

"Hold on."

Ruth got out of the car and walked around to the pole. She looked at Senem and smiled. She raised her thumb in the air.

"Not even a scratch!" she called. Then she looked at the grass. "No damage to the grass, either."

This time, Senem got the car into reverse and then slowly backed out into the street. Ruth cheered, and Senem joined her.

"Yahoo! Hooray! We did it!"

"Now," said Senem. "Lesson is finished. We will go to my home and drink tea. You drive."

"Enough fun for one day," Ruth agreed.

Senem's Journal, Wednesday, July 21

I want to tell you a little story about my American friend Ruth. You know her. You met her at my house. She is very nice woman. Her son is friend of Hasan. Ruth is teaching me to drive a car. When Hasan and the son of Ruth are in preschool, we drive in her car in quiet part of the city. It is exciting. The first time, I was too nervous. The second time, I crashed car into light pole. I didn't hurt car! Now, I am getting better. In Turkey, I did not drive because traffic was terrible. Here, I think I can learn. When I return to Turkey, I can have more freedom because I will drive. Maybe Tarkan and I can be able to buy a house and I will drive to my job in the downtown Ankara.

Karen's Response

Ruth is a nice friend. I would like to hear more about your job in downtown Ankara. Is traffic terrible because there are too many cars or because no one follows the traffic rules? When I lived in Mexico City, traffic was crazy. If there was a traffic jam going one way, the cars would drive into the oncoming lanes and cause a traffic jam going the other way, too! No one followed the traffic laws. On the other hand, in New York traffic is bad because there are so many vehicles on the narrow streets.

After English class, Ruth picked up Senem and Hasan. Hasan and Jeremy went to a birthday party for a pre-school friend, and Ruth took Senem for another driving lesson. They had been practicing for several weeks. Ruth was a good teacher. She was patient and thorough. Senem felt better about her driving now, but Ruth noticed something was wrong.

"What's the matter, Senem? You seem distracted."

Senem pulled over to the curb and stopped the car.

"I cannot stop thinking about many talks with Tarkan."

"You mean talks like arguments? Tell me about it."

"Tarkan want me to have baby now. He is right. It will be better to do now. In Turkey is difficult because I will work."

"So what's the problem?" asked Ruth.

"I am afraid."

"Why?"

"So many things! I am afraid I can't keep two children safe. Also, when I was pregnant of Hasan, I all the time feel so sick. And when he borned, it was very difficult and long. Thirty-six hours of. . . ." Senem put her hands on her belly.

"Labor. Oh gosh, Senem. That must have been awful. Mine was easy in comparison. I was in hard labor for three hours with Jeremy, and then, boom, out he came. Is that what you are worried about? That your labor will last a long time?"

"Yes, and also, I do not have my mother and sisters here to help me. It will be too hard to have new baby and take care of Hasan. I have to watch Hasan very carefully now. I know now he can be taken from me."

"But I'm here, Senem. And Martha, and Karen, and the students in your class. And the other students at the University. We are your family here. We'll help you. Don't worry anymore about that!"

Senem did worry, though. She was still not sure that having another baby was the best idea. But Ruth's words were comforting. She did have a little family here in the U.S. It was not exactly like her big, friendly, and noisy family in Turkey. There, everyone in the family understood her perfectly. She understood them, too. No, this new family was not the same, but it was almost as good.

CHAPTER 6

Senem's Journal, Monday, August 2

When I came to Denver last year, I thought "What will I do for two years? I'm alone. I don't have any friends or relatives here." So I was sad and lonely.

Now, I never feel like this. Because you, Martha, and Ruth are here. I love all of you so much.

Some Turkish people don't want to return to Turkey. Because the life is here better and easier than Turkey. They want to live in Denver forever. I don't think like them. I will be happy when I return to Turkey. Because it is my country even it is hard to live there. But now I feel that, when I return to Turkey I can't be happy like I thought. Because I will leave from you.

I will be in Denver for eleven months more. I can say anytime what I feel. But I want to say that now, I will never forget, especially you and Martha and Ruth.

Karen's Response

It has been wonderful for me to have you in class. I will always remember your smiling face and interesting journal entries. It's fun to hear about all you do with Martha and Ruth and your other friends. You have such fun together. I wish I had more free time to spend with you. I enjoyed the picnics in the park during the summer. Luckily, you have eleven more months here. I'm not ready to say goodbye!

Senem, Ruth, and Martha agreed that the hottest August afternoons were perfect for cooking lessons. They would meet once a week at someone's house and learn how to make a dish from Turkey, Mexico, or the U.S.

"I want to learn how to make stuffed grape leaves first," said Ruth.

"Oh, yes, delicious!" Martha agreed.

"Okay, we'll make sarma," said Senem. "We'll cook my house first."

"Hmm, cooked house. Not too tasty," said Ruth.

Martha and Senem just looked at her.

"Kidding! I'm kidding!" laughed Ruth. "Seriously, let's cook at my house first. I have a new kitchen. We can make grape leaves in my new kitchen. Do you want to come Friday afternoon while the kids are in pre-school?"

Ruth said that she could prepare a few ingredients before the lesson, and Senem said she would call Ruth with the directions.

Thursday evening she called Ruth. "I think you will make rice, okay?" asked Senem.

"Okay," said Ruth. "Is there a special way you cook it?"

"Um, broil rice."

"Broil it?"

"Yes. Soak plain white rice in water for 30 minutes and then broil it with onion, tomato paste, and lemon."

"Wow," said Ruth. "Not **boil,** but **broil**?"

"Yes, don't boil. Broil."

"Okay, you're the boss. I'll have broiled rice waiting for you!"

"Tarkan, how do Americans make rice?" Senem asked Tarkan when she hung up the phone.

"The same way we do, I suppose," he said.

"I don't think so," said Senem.

"Senem, do you realize what you were doing?"

"What?"

"You were talking on the telephone in English."

"You're right! I didn't even worry about it!"

Tarkan smiled. *"Hmm. Now that you can speak English, what about having another baby?"*

"What? How are the two things related?"

"Well, now you can talk to the doctors, and you have friends to help you, and you're not working. It's perfect."

Senem walked toward the bedroom. Tarkan followed her. *"Is that a yes?"* he asked.

"It's a maybe," said Senem, with a laugh. *"And don't you have homework to do?"*

❖

On Friday afternoon, Senem and Martha walked into Ruth's kitchen carrying bags with grape leaves in jars and other things they needed to make the stuffed grape leaves. There was a funny smell in the kitchen. It smelled like something had burned.

Ruth took a shallow pan out of the refrigerator. She set the pan on the counter.

"Come and look," she said. "This doesn't seem right."

Martha and Senem looked into the pan. It was full of gooey pink and gray rice with a crisp black top.

"Oh!" said Martha. She raised her eyebrows and looked at Senem.

"What is it?" asked Senem.

"Broiled rice," said Ruth. "I followed your instructions. You said to soak the rice in water and then broil it for 20 minutes."

Senem looked around the kitchen. She saw some pots and pans hanging from a holder on the ceiling. She took one down. "This kind of pan," she said. She put the pan on a burner on top of the stove. "You cooked like this? With olive oil and other things I told you?"

Ruth began to laugh. "No! I used the broiler!" She opened the oven. She pointed to the heating element at the top of the oven. "I used the broiler."

All the women began to laugh.

"I thought it was a strange way to cook rice!" said Ruth.

Senem turned on the heat under the pan. "If I put rice, onion, tomato paste, lemon here, and cook with stirring, what is the word for this?"

"Sauté! What an airhead I am!" laughed Ruth. "Oh, Senem, I'm sorry, I should have figured it out! I just thought, well, those Turkish people sure make weird rice!"

Senem and Martha smiled at each other.

"Ruth, we have confession," said Martha, "Senem call me about rice. She say me to soak some rice in water, too. She was worry you no make it good!"

She reached into her bag and pulled out a bowl of soaked white rice.

"Let's make sarma," Senem said. The three friends got to work, laughing, talking, and cooking together.

The good times with her friends helped lessen Senem's nightmares. But they didn't take them away completely. She still dreamed about Hasan being kidnapped. But one night, she dreamed she was back in Ankara, her home city, and there was another earthquake, only much bigger. All the buildings crumbled to dust. She was left standing in the middle of a city of rubble. She cried and screamed for Tarkan, Hasan, her mother, and her sisters. She awoke when Tarkan shook her by the shoulder.

"Senem, Senem, wake up! You're crying in your sleep! Wake up."

She rolled over and put her arms around Tarkan.

"Another bad dream?" he asked.

"Yes. It was terrible. There was a big earthquake in Turkey. It seemed real." Tears streamed down her face.

Tarkan hugged her and rubbed her back, but she could not calm down.

"Let's look at the news," he said, finally. *"You'll see, everything is fine in Turkey. It's almost time to get up, anyway."*

Tarkan and Senem went into the living room. They turned on the television, and Tarkan changed the channel from cartoons to an all-news channel.

They were surprised to see Senem's nightmare suddenly there, on TV. Somewhere in the world there had been an earthquake. Clouds of dust rose from mounds of debris. Emergency workers in hard hats were digging in the remains of buildings. Injured men, women, and children walked aimlessly through the ruined buildings and buckled streets.

Senem gasped and leaned into Tarkan so he could hold her. A strange fear came over her. *"Where is it?"* she asked.

"I don't know," said Tarkan.

A reporter started to talk, and all at once she realized what he was saying: "All of northwestern Turkey is in ruins. You can see behind me all that is left of a residential section of Izmit, near the epicenter of the terrible quake."

Izmit! Izmit was an industrial city about 100 miles west of Ankara. Senem's family was in Ankara, far from the epicenter, but Hulya, her dear oldest sister, was in Izmit. She was at her annual dance camp. And, she realized, that was where Emine was in jail. She was waiting to be transferred to a larger women's prison. In addition, Senem's grandparents lived in a big house in Gemlik. It was very close to the epicenter of the earthquake, which was in the Marmara Sea. Tarkan's family lived in Istanbul, which was only 55 miles east of Izmit. The reporter kept talking, and a map filled the TV screen.

Tarkan and Senem sat on the sofa in their living room. They held hands and watched the terrible news. Tarkan tried to call their parents in Turkey, but the lines were all busy. The reporter said that hundreds, maybe thousands, of buildings collapsed in the earthquake. Thousands of people were certainly dead.

Senem felt numb. She listened to the reporter.

"The earthquake occurred at 3:02 AM local time, as most of the area's residents were asleep in their beds," she said. "It lasted 45 seconds—45 seconds of terror—and, as the dust clears, rescue operations are underway for the many people who are trapped. The U.K., the U.S.A., France, Germany, and Japan are all rushing emergency supplies and rescue workers to the area."

❖

All day their Turkish friends came over. By the afternoon, the apartment was full of people. The TV was tuned to the news, and Tarkan searched the Internet every few minutes for information. People spent all day trying to get through to Turkey on cell phones or on Tarkan and Senem's phone. No one wanted to go home without news about their families.

Finally, one friend was able to reach his mother. He held his hand up for silence as she told him of the horror. No one in his family was hurt, but many friends had lost their homes.

In the evening, Senem and some of the other women prepared a meal for everyone in the apartment. They were sitting down to eat when the phone rang. Tarkan jumped up to answer it. His face beamed with joy.

"It's my father!" he told the people in the room.

"Everyone in my family is okay! Our house is still standing."

His friends cheered, and he continued talking to his father for a few minutes more. When he hung up, Senem went to his side. *"Do they know about my family?"* she asked quietly. *"Did my mother or father call them?"*

"Not yet. But everything is in chaos there. They estimate that 20,000 people are dead."

Eventually, their friends talked to parents and friends and learned that they were okay. One woman's house collapsed, but her family got out with only minor injuries. One man's grandfather was missing. One by one, people went home to wait for more phone calls. Finally, only Hasan, Tarkan, and Senem remained in their small apartment. They were exhausted. Senem still did not know about her family.

"I'll put Hasan to bed," she said.

"I'll try to call your parents one more time," said Tarkan.

"Thank you," said Senem and kissed him on the cheek. She carried Hasan to his room, tucked him in, and sang him a soft lullaby. He was asleep before she finished.

When she returned to the living room, Tarkan was talking quietly on the telephone. He looked up at her. Once again, she felt that strange, cold fear in her stomach. *"What is it?"* she asked.

Tarkan handed her the telephone. It was her mother. *"Senem, we are all safe in Ankara. We only felt a little tremor. But your grandparents' house collapsed. They are safe, but they lost everything."*

"Oh, Mama, that's terrible. But they are fine? They are not hurt?"

"Yes." Senem heard her mother's voice shake. *"We have more bad news. Hulya was in Izmit. We know the building she was living in collapsed."* There was a pause before she said, *"She's still missing."*

Senem and her mother were both crying when Tarkan gently took the telephone.

"We'll call you again later," he said. He hung up. Senem fell into his arms and wept.

CHAPTER 7

That night, for the first time since the kidnapping, Senem didn't check on Hasan in the night. But, Hasan came into their bedroom in the early morning. *"What's the matter, Mommy? Your eyes are all funny and red."*

"Hasan, come here," said his father gently. Hasan climbed up on the bed next to Tarkan. *"Do you remember all the people who came over yesterday?"*

Hasan nodded.

"There was a big earthquake in Turkey, and we were all very worried. Grandma called last night. Mommy's sad because no one can find Aunt Hulya."

When Hasan saw Senem's eyes filled with tears, he leaned over and gave her a kiss on her cheek as she had done to him a thousand times.

"Let's let Mommy try to sleep. Come with me, and I'll make you some breakfast." Tarkan picked up Hasan and took him into the kitchen.

Senem stayed in bed. Tarkan took her some tea and bread. Senem drank a few sips of tea and ate one or two bites of bread, but that's all she could manage. After a couple of hours, she got up and went into the living room. Hasan was watching TV, and Tarkan was reading the newspaper. Senem sat on the couch beside them.

"Who called this morning?" she asked. *"I heard the phone ring."*

"Ruth called. She made some food and wants to bring it over. She saw the news on TV."

"That's nice of her," Senem said. *"But I want to keep busy. People might be coming over. I will cook some food, too, and make tea."*

Tarkan nodded. *"I'll take Hasan to the park for a little while,"* he said. *"We need to get outside. It's a nice, sunny day."*

"*Don't forget the sunscreen,*" said Senem. She turned on TV news and turned up the volume. Then she went into the kitchen and started getting some ingredients out of the cupboards. She heard the announcer describing the scenes of devastation in Izmit. When she heard a voice in Turkish, she left her cooking to see who was talking.

A young woman was sobbing, her face in her hands. The interviewer was leaning forward intently, trying to record her words. The translator slowly started translating what she was saying.

"I was coming back from a party with some friends after our performance. We were two blocks away, near the park, when the earth began to shake. We screamed and ran into a clearing. The buildings began to topple. The noise was terrible. My friends and I realized the building our dance troupe

was living in had collapsed. We didn't know what to do. We ran in the direction everyone was running. Then, when the shaking stopped, we stopped."

The woman took a deep breath and raised her face to the camera. Senem gasped. Looking straight at the camera, the woman said, *"My friends and I joined a team of people helping to rescue survivors. There were so many wounded people. But now, I want to say to my family, I am okay. I am not hurt."* It was Hulya!

The reporter was excited. "You haven't contacted your family yet? This is their first news that you are okay?"

Hulya, Senem's sister, her beautiful face dirty and streaked with tears, nodded. *"To my parents and sisters and whole family, I am fine. I'll stay here to help. They shouldn't worry about me."*

Senem ran to the television and placed her hands on Hulya's beloved face. Quickly, the picture changed to the interviewer. She was saying that helping people communicate in such bad times was one of the most rewarding parts of her job. Senem just wanted to see her sister, to take in her face with her eyes. The reporter kept on talking, though, so Senem threw on her sweater and rushed out of the apartment.

On the way down the stairs, she met some of Tarkan's friends. Laughing, she handed them the keys to the apartment. *"Go on in! Have some tea! My sister has been found. I'm going to tell Tarkan."*

Tarkan and Hasan were playing in the small grassy park near the apartment. They were kicking a soccer ball back and forth. Tarkan laughed as Hasan tried to give the ball mighty kicks. *"Good, kick it again,"* he said. He looked up when Senem called his name.

Tarkan could see by the smile on Senem's face that something good had happened. He smiled, too, and ran toward her. Hasan ran up, too, and all three ended up in a little circle. They were laughing. Senem picked up Hasan. *"Aunt Hulya is fine! She's alive and not injured!"*

"Yay!" screamed Hasan. He was intoxicated by their dancing, by his parents' joy. He didn't know Aunt Hulya. He was just happy that Mommy and Daddy were happy.

"Thank God," said Tarkan, with relief. *"Everyone is fine."*

"Oh, and some friends are at the apartment. We should all go back," said Senem. Laughing and talking, they crossed the street and entered the apartment building. As they opened the door to the apartment, the phone was ringing. While Tarkan greeted his friends, Senem answered the phone. It was her mother. *"Senem! Good news! Hulya is fine. She is not hurt! She just called us,"* cried her mother.

"I saw her on television," said Senem. *"It was a miracle. I heard a voice speaking Turkish, and I went out of the kitchen to see what was happening, and it was Hulya! At first she had her face hidden, but I*

knew there was something familiar about her. And then, there she was!"

Senem and her mother talked a little longer, the relief making both of them giddy. Then Senem's mother said, *"There is more news, though. That woman, Emine. The one in jail—"*

"Yes?"

"She's in the hospital. Her cell block was destroyed, and she was injured."

"Oh, no. Was she badly hurt?"

"I don't know, Senem. It's strange. Her mother was confused. She kept saying the injuries might not kill her, but I'm afraid for her life."

"That is strange," said Senem. *"What did she mean?"*

"Well, she said something about Emine not eating in prison. She just lay in her bed with her face to the wall, day and night."

Senem and her mother talked some more. The news about Emine saddened her. She wondered what she could do. She got the hospital telephone number from her mother and hung up.

Tarkan noticed her sitting by the phone. He left his friends and sat with her. *"What's wrong?"* he asked.

"It's Emine."

He frowned. *"Let's not talk about her."*

"I'm sorry to bring it up. My mother told me she hasn't eaten for several days. She was injured in the earthquake, but not badly. Even so, she's in the hos-

pital. Her mother seems to think she's dying."

"Are you sure?"

Senem looked at Tarkan in surprise. *"I hope you don't mean you're pleased about this."*

Tarkan looked down at his hands. *"Oh, no, of course not. It's just that, no matter what, Emine comes up. We should be celebrating, and here you are, worrying about a woman who kidnapped our son. I'm glad you're a compassionate person—"*

"—but you're tired of it," said Senem, finishing his sentence for him.

Tarkan shrugged. Senem stood up. She went into the kitchen to finish the cooking she had started earlier. She thought about Emine. Had Emine lost the will to live? Was this Senem's fault? Did she miss signs that Emine was too attached to Hasan? No, she decided. That was ridiculous. She could not take responsibility for what happened or for Emine's reaction. That didn't mean she shouldn't try to help Emine, though. She decided to enjoy the afternoon with Tarkan, Hasan, and the friends who were at the apartment. Then, tomorrow, she would call Emine and try to make her feel better.

❖

The next day Ruth picked up Hasan for pre-school, and Tarkan went to work. Senem had a little time before her English class at 9 AM. If she called Emine now, it would be late afternoon in Turkey. She dialed the number of the hospital where Emine was being treated.

A woman answered. Her voice was deep. The combination of the deep voice and the static on the line made her difficult to understand. Senem asked for Emine Bahar. The woman said something Senem didn't quite hear.

"Pardon me?" Senem asked.

"That young woman died this morning," said the woman in a loud voice. *"Her relatives have already taken her away."*

Senem whispered a shaky "*thank you*" into the phone and hung up. She sat down on the sofa and wept. Very soon, she heard a knock at the door. Martha. She had forgotten about Martha. She had come to Senem's so they could walk to class together. Senem wiped her face and went to the door. When she opened it, Martha could see something was wrong. "Senem, what happened?" she asked.

Martha knew the whole story. She knew that Emine was in jail in Turkey and that Alex was in jail in the U.S. She knew that Tarkan was still angry with Emine, and that he blamed her for Senem's reluctance to get pregnant. Now, Senem told her about Emine's hunger strike. She told her that Emine was dead.

"I think I cannot go to class—," said Senem.

"I understand, Senem. You feel so sad because Emine was your friend. Maybe she a little crazy, but is not change how you feel for her. Is no same, but my grandmother died last year in Mexico. I was so sad. We have no money for me to go for the funeral. I am then very sad, how do you say, depressed? I not go for school three weeks. Karen come to my apartment and ask for me to come back. Then is better, little by little."

"I'm sorry about your grandmother," said Senem. "I will think about what you say. Thank you."

"I going now," said Martha. "But I be back tomorrow for the school. You coming then."

Senem smiled. "Maybe," she said. After she closed the door she thought about Emine. She remembered how much Hasan loved her. She remembered cooking with her, watching television with her, laughing with her. Then she thought of her sister, Hulya. Emine was dead, but Hulya was alive. How did those two things go together? One was so joyous, the other was so terrible. She lost track of time, just sitting and thinking. The doorbell rang again. Hasan was home from preschool already.

Ruth brought the boys in the door. Hasan and Jeremy immediately ran off to Hasan's room. Ruth handed Senem a large bunch of flowers. "Look what I found at the grocery store! Sunflowers!"

"Oh, Ruth, you make me smile," said Senem gratefully. "This is Emine's favorite flower. She always have . . . had yellow color—a scarf or blouse.

And her bedroom in her apartment was paint . . . painted, all yellow. So happy."

"Emine? Why are you thinking about her?"

Senem told Ruth the news. She told her about her confused feelings about Hulya and Emine.

The two women sat on the sofa for almost an hour. Senem brought out a small photo album and told Ruth stories of her childhood in Turkey.

"I love hearing about this, Senem," Ruth said. "Anytime you want to talk, just call me. I'm only a phone call away. And don't just call when you are okay. Call when you're sad and angry, too, if you can. It's important. You're not alone here." She took a paper out of her handbag. "Look, I have this information about grief. I got it from the Internet. It tells you what to expect when a loved one dies. I got it when I first heard Hulya was missing, but it might help you with Emine. If you want to talk about it, call me."

"Thank you, Ruth. I'll read it. But is so difficult."

"You bet it is. Take your time. Everyone is different. Let yourself cry. Grief is a 100 percent experience. No one does it at 50 percent."

Somehow Senem made it through the long afternoon. Finally, Tarkan came home. When he walked in, she couldn't stand her sorrow anymore. She put her arms around him and began to cry. He held her and kissed her hair as she whispered through her tears that Emine was dead.

"I love you, Senem," was all he said. He led her to the bedroom and helped her get into bed. *"Sleep."*

❖

When Senem woke up, it was still dark outside: 3:12 AM. She heard Tarkan snoring lightly next to her.

No tears came. Her mind was calm and clear. She thought back over the past year and how her life had changed. Thanks to Ruth, Karen, Martha, and the other students in the English class, her English had really improved. She and her husband and son had seen some wonderful parts of this big country. She had been betrayed by a trusted friend and almost lost Hasan. While parts of her country were destroyed by an earthquake, she sat, safe, in her living room in Denver. And now, her friend was dead. She reflected on her disagreements with Tarkan and her own indecision about having another child.

Then an amazing thing happened. There in the darkness, she felt a warmth. Her mind was filled with a golden light. Senem thought of Hulya. She was alive, helping others in Turkey. She thought of Emine. It seemed like she was in the room. Not Emine as she had been at the end, confused and tormented. She thought of the other Emine. The energetic, positive, sunny Emine who had loved Hasan.

Slowly, the feeling disappeared like an early morning mist. Senem lay still. She no longer felt indecisive. Emine was dead, but Hulya was alive. Senem would always remember her friend and carry the good, positive memories of her in her heart. She was not going to spend her life afraid. Life must go on. Senem knew there would be bad days and good days ahead. But now she had hope. She and Tarkan would renew their faith in life by bringing a new life into the world. She was ready now to have another baby.

CHAPTER 8

Senem's Journal, Monday, November 1

I am not feeling good. I am feeling very sick. I can tell you now a secret. I am pregnant! Tarkan and I decided now is good for us to have a second child. It was hard decision for us to make, but we decided now is time to live. Now is a time for new beginning. He or she will come in early July, before we go back to Turkey. I am excited (and Tarkan is proud), but I miss my mother. She was all the time with me in Turkey and made my life so easy while I was pregnant with Hasan. Now I have Hasan to take care, and I can not rest all the time I want to. I am a big complaining person!

Karen's Response

WOW! Congratulations. If you need anything or any help taking care of Hasan, please let me know. Do you want me to keep this a secret, or do you want to let the class know about it? A big complaining person is a "whiner." You aren't a whiner!

After she read Senem's journal, Karen went to the classroom's storage closet. She came back with a package of saltine crackers that the pre-school kids sometimes ate for a snack. She handed them to Senem.

"When I was pregnant with my son, I ate these all the time," she whispered. "They really help."

"Hey, Senem have a food," said Carmen loudly. "She still Karen's favorite, no?"

Karen smiled, looked at Senem, and raised her eyebrows. "Well?" she asked.

"Okay," Senem laughed. "I will tell all the class my new secret."

"I like secrets very much," said Carmen.

"I make a riddle," said Senem. "I know Carmen like riddles."

Carmen said, "I don't know what is riddles. How can I like it?"

Senem looked at Karen. "A riddle is a joke, a joke you guess, right?"

"Right," said Karen.

Senem thought for a minute. Then she said, "What makes you sick and still you get fat even you can't eat?"

Karen wrote it on the board: "What makes you so sick that you can't eat, but you still get fat?" She drew a picture of a stick woman with a sickly look on her face and a big stomach.

Everyone laughed. Natasha, the Ukrainian student, said, "I guess you will have a baby! I will be the American grandmother!"

Carmen said, "Oh, a baby, okay you can have a food every day. You feel sick, eh?"

All the students talked and laughed at the same time. Senem was surprised at the excited response from her English class. They all behaved as if she was a close relative, and her new child belonged to all of them.

Flor said something to her in Spanish.

"Flor, Senem doesn't speak Spanish!" laughed Karen. "Try that in English."

"I wish you good, happy, easy time," said Flor slowly. Senem thanked her. Flor smiled and nodded her head.

"When I am pregnant, I never sick," announced Carmen proudly. "But now I have two babies, boy and girl. I never try that again!"

"Why?" asked Natasha.

"Too much hurt!"

Karen rephrased it. "It hurts too much."

"Yes, that's right!" said Carmen.

The students laughed again, and Senem munched on a cracker. She was glad that she shared her secret with the class.

❖

Unfortunately, this good feeling didn't last for a very long time. Senem was so tired and sick to her stomach. Everything she smelled—Ruth's perfume, the flowers Martha brought for her, the oil heating in a pan—made her feel sick, although she never threw up. Sometimes, though, she wished she could just throw up. Then she might feel better.

Every day after class she took a nap. She was grateful that Hasan went to pre-school because it was hard to sleep with him in the apartment. She loved sleeping. The nightmares were gone. She had wonderful dreams. Sometimes she dreamed that she was flying, and sometimes she and her sister Hulya were dancing to old Turkish songs. Once she dreamed that she was an opera singer and that millions of people adored her.

She made these dreams into stories for Hasan. He loved them and listened quietly. As soon as she was done telling the story, though, he wanted to play.

She told Ruth how tired she was and how hard it was to entertain Hasan.

"All I love is sleeping," she said. "I never want to wake up."

"I always had to take a nap when I was pregnant, too," said Ruth. "You know what you should do? Make your life easier. Look around your apartment. Are there things you do out of habit that you don't really need to do? Look at yourself. What could you change about your morning routine? Look at the way you cook. Could you buy some things ready-made? Honey, I learned long ago to simplify."

"Give me one example from your life," said Senem.

"Okay, don't tell anyone, but I never clean under the furniture."

"You mean you never move sofa and clean floor there?"

"Never."

"It will get so dirty!"

"Who cares? I never see it. Someday, when we get a new sofa, I can clean under the old one when we move it out of the house."

"I am sorry, Ruth, but that is terrible."

Ruth laughed. "Okay, okay, maybe that's not the tip for you, but find some things you could give up!"

Senem thought carefully about her daily routine. One thing she was finding so tiresome was taking care of her hair. She had long, thick, wavy hair that fell to her shoulders. When it was dirty, she got up early to wash and condition it and then blow it dry. It took at least 45 minutes. Every six weeks Tarkan trimmed it for her, and then she had to clean up the hair from the floor of the bathroom.

"My hair is a lot of work," she muttered, as she brushed it out of her eyes.

One day, while Hasan was in pre-school, she skipped her nap. Instead, she went to a small beauty salon she passed on the way to class. Through the window she saw two people getting their hair cut. She walked in. A young woman with

Beauty Salon

purple hair was reading a magazine. When Senem came in, she put the magazine down and smiled.

"What can I do for you?" she asked.

"I can have a hair cut?" asked Senem.

"Sure. Wash and a cut or just a cut?"

"Just a cut. Cut it short."

Later, at home, she looked at her face in the mirror. Her hair was very short, not just a little short. She looked like a little girl. Her bangs were spiky. Her eyes looked very big, and her neck looked so long. She heard Ruth, Jeremy, and Hasan come in the door.

"Mama, Mama, I'm home!" shouted Hasan, in English.

Senem walked to the end of the hall and held out her arms for a hug from Hasan. He came running, but suddenly he stopped.

"Mama! You turned into a boy!"

Ruth said, "Senem, what did you do?"

"I cut off my hair," said Senem. She felt a little silly.

"Are you a boy?" repeated Hasan.

Senem knelt down. *"No, of course not. I just wanted a change. I wanted short hair, like you."*

"But I am a boy."

Senem put her arms around him. *"Do you like my short hair?"*

He looked into her face. *"It is beautiful,"* he said seriously. *"But I wish you were a boy now."*

Senem smiled. *"I'm sorry, I'm still the same old Mama."*

After Ruth and Jeremy left, Senem told Hasan a story and then called Denver Health to make her first prenatal appointment. Before she got pregnant, she and Tarkan went to Denver Health and bought health insurance under a special program for low-income families. All they had to do was show that they had only a small income from the Turkish government and proof that they were in the United States legally.

Senem thought back to the class discussion about health care a few weeks ago. Many of the people in her class did not have insurance because they had small incomes and were in the United States illegally. She remembered asking at Denver Health what would happen if the family were in the country illegally.

"We would still treat you," the insurance agent said. "But it would be more expensive."

When they lived in Turkey and Senem worked for the public sector, her health care was almost free. In Turkey, she could go to a public hospital and pay nothing. In the U.S., even with insurance, she would pay for part of everything. After Senem made the appointment, she felt tired. When Hasan wanted to play, Senem decided to try something based on Ruth's advice.

"Hasan, I have something special for you," she said. *"But you can only play with it while I'm resting.*

When I'm not resting, we have to put it away."

Hasan was very excited. Senem got a bag out of the closet. In the bag were a big block of clay; some plastic sculpting tools; and a set of small eyes, ears, feet, hats, hands, and mustaches. She helped Hasan set everything out on the kitchen table.

"Now remember, you can only play with this while I rest. As soon as I get up, we have to put it all away."

Hasan nodded. *"Have a long rest, Mama,"* he said. *"I have a lot to do."*

Hasan loved the clay, and he didn't disturb Senem at all. When Tarkan came home an hour later, Senem was still resting. Hasan showed Tarkan ten little men with strange combinations of body parts and hats. *"Don't bother Mama, or I have to stop playing,"* he whispered. *"And don't be surprised, she almost turned into a boy."*

Tarkan went in and kissed Senem on the cheek. She opened her eyes and rolled to face him. He raised his eyebrows.

"Is this your new look?"

Senem put her hand on her short, short hair. *"Do you like it?"*

Tarkan looked at her carefully. *"Are you a boy now? Because boys can't have babies."*

Senem's Journal, Friday, November 12

I like my new haircut. Tarkan thinks it is fine for now, but after the baby is born, he thinks I must have longer hair again. Short hair is part of simplifying my life! It is strange to say that because here I have the easy life. In Turkey, I am so busy with my job and my family. I will learn to enjoy this quiet life.

Karen's Response

Your hair looks beautiful. I'll bet that just as you learn to enjoy this life, you'll leave for Turkey. It's so hard to appreciate what you have while you have it.

Senem's Journal, Monday, November 15

When the earthquake happened in Turkey, I felt awful. I was so sad about all the people who died and lost their relatives. My sister lived, but then Emine died. I feel so bad about that all the time. Last Friday, an earthquake happened again. It was like a nightmare. My sister called me as soon as possible, and she said to me, "Don't worry, my mom, dad, and all other relatives are safe." After she called me I was getting better. But then I think to myself and I felt that I was selfish. So many people died again, and I thought first of my mom and dad.

Karen's Response

What terrible news. Turkey has had enough tragedy. I don't think you were selfish to think first of your parents. It's a natural reaction, and we always care most about those who we love. My parents live in Los Angeles. Whenever there is an earthquake there, I call them immediately. Then I worry about others. Also, you know people in that big earthquake! Of course you worry about your family. I put underlines in a few places where there are grammar problems. Can you figure out the correct forms?

CHAPTER 9

Senem's Journal, Monday, March 27

Today I am very happy for two reasons. The first reason is that we received two invitation _by_ Easter dinner, one from my American friend, Ruth, and one from a Turkish friend. Now I don't know what we will decide. Perhaps we will go both places, but I can not eat two times! There is something in my stomach already, and I have no room.

Karen laughed out loud when she read this. "Here we say, 'Have some more food. Now you are eating for two.' Has anyone said this to you?"

Senem nodded. "Yes, yesterday in the doctor's office. Someone I do not know."

"That is common. Everyone loves to see a pregnant woman. Don't be surprised if people reach out and touch your belly now that you're showing."

"Showing, what is this?" asked Senem.

"When the baby grows and people can see that you are pregnant." Karen gestured with her hands.

"It is so much fun to follow your baby's development."

"My development, too," Senem joked. Karen laughed again.

"Right!"

The second reason is my old__ sister, Hulya, will come near __ end of May. I received the letter yesterday. She will stay until July and be with us when we return to Turkey.

Karen's Response

That is very exciting news! Please bring her to class. She can join us while she is here. I underlined a few mistakes. See if you can figure them out.

Lessons at school were mostly about spring. Senem remembered many things from the year before, but she understood the discussions more easily. She was able to participate and ask and answer questions more fluently without using her Turkish/English dictionary to translate words so often.

Senem was interested in the religious part of Easter. Karen did a whole lesson on the story of Holy Week and the death of Jesus.

"Why you no celebrate Easter in Turkey?" asked Carmen.

"We are Muslims. Our religion is Islam, not Christian. For us, Jesus is important prophet, but not the most important person. That is Mohammed."

Senem explained that at their apartment they dyed eggs with Hasan's American friends. Then, they all hunted for the Easter eggs together. Here in the United States they enjoyed the cultural holiday.

"When in Rome, do as the Romans do," said Karen. "Does everyone understand?"

"Is when somebody are at a place not their own, they act like the peoples in that place, not like in their home?" Martha asked.

"Yes, that's it. Senem doesn't celebrate Easter in Turkey, but now that she's here, she participates in some American holidays and traditions."

Ruth's Easter invitation was for noon, and the other one wasn't until 6:00 PM, so Senem, Tarkan, and Hasan went to both.

Senem went in the kitchen to see if Ruth needed help.

"Nope," said Ruth. "We're all ready to sit down. My mom came over at 8:00 this morning, and we've been cooking up a storm."

Senem looked out the window. It was a breezy, cool spring day, but the sun was shining and the sky was mostly blue.

"Storm? I don't see storm. The weather is nice outside."

"Oh, Senem, not that kind of storm. 'Cooking up a storm' is an expression. It means doing a lot of cooking. We roasted a leg of lamb. And we cooked mashed potatoes, gravy, rolls, and peas, and we made a salad and mint sauce," Ruth said, counting each item off on her fingers. "Oh, and yesterday I made strawberry shortcake and hot cross buns from scratch."

"From scratch?" asked Senem.

"Yes. I bought the ingredients at the store, but then I made everything here at home."

"Oh. I think all food in Turkey is made from scratch."

"You're lucky. There are too many preservatives in American food. Home-made is so much healthier."

There were 12 people around the table, including Ruth's parents, sister, and niece, Ruth's father-in-law, and brother. The men were watching basketball on TV, but they were hungry and happy to come to the table after smelling the delicious smells coming from the kitchen all morning.

The get-together at their Turkish friend's apartment was very different. The other guests were all graduate students and their spouses. It was a potluck, so everyone brought a dish from their country. Senem didn't think she would be hungry after the feast at Ruth's, but she took a small helping of everything. She surprised herself by finishing it all.

❖

April passed quickly. Now in her seventh month, Senem didn't have morning sickness anymore. She told the class what happened at her check-ups every other week.

"The nurse take my blood pressure and weigh me. Then she listen to my breath in my chest and back. Then she listen with special tool and she hear heartbeat of my baby. And I listen, too. It is so exciting."

"You hear your baby every time?" asked Carmen. "Is make you feel so good, yes?"

"Yes, is true," said Senem. "And last week I also saw pictures of my baby. Is called ultrasound. I had same in Turkey with Hasan."

"Did you find out if your baby is a boy or a girl?" asked Karen.

"Oh no! I do not want to know."

"Then we will not know to buy pink or blue clothes," said Carmen.

"What do you mean?" asked Senem.

"Oops," said Carmen. "I think I spoil the surprise."

Senem was very confused now.

"It's okay," said Karen. "Senem, we were talking before you came in today that we want to give you a baby shower. We decided to wait until the end of May. That way you can think of what you want and need for the baby. And, your sister will be here then. And it will still be more than a month until your baby is due at the end of June, so you won't be so tired."

Senem was smiling, but she wasn't sure what a baby shower was. She guessed it was a kind of party when people brought presents for the baby.

Karen looked around the room. "Does everyone understand? Flor, do you understand?"

Flor smiled shyly. "This shower?" She made motions of scrubbing her shoulder with her hand.

"Yes," said Karen, "That is a shower, but a baby shower is different. Can anyone explain?"

"This is shower of presents, not water," said a student. Flor looked more confused.

"What are presents?" asked Karen.

"You give something to somebody," said Martha.

"Yes," Karen repeated. She drew a picture on the board of a box with a bow. Next to it, she drew a baby.

Flor smiled broadly. "I understand." She pointed at the board. "Presents. They for the Senem baby."

❖

A month later, on a warm day in May, Tarkan, Senem, and Hasan drove out to Denver International Airport. They parked the car and went to the baggage area. Senem's sister, Hulya, was already there. Senem called her name.

"Is that you, Senem? Your hair is so short!" Hulya cried as she hugged Senem tightly and kissed her on both cheeks.

"She looks like a boy, doesn't she, Auntie Hulya?" said Hasan.

"Well, maybe a little." She picked up Hasan and showered him with kisses. *"But you are really a boy! A big, big boy!"*

Hasan giggled and wiggled. When Hulya put him down, he ran to Senem, still laughing.

After more hugs for Tarkan and many kisses, they all walked to the car. Senem and Hulya walked arm-in-arm.

"Mommy, why are you crying?" asked Hasan.

"They are tears of joy. I'm so happy that your auntie is here."

Hulya told them all about the 20-hour flight from Ankara.

"I was so glad that the flight from Ankara to Frankfurt was not delayed. If it had been, I never would have made the connection in Chicago!" she said. *"I had to run anyway."*

She was too tired to answer Senem's questions about their family in any detail. *"They all send their love and look forward to July when we go back."*

Hulya was visiting because she wanted to be with Senem when the baby was born. Also, she needed to be away from the rebuilding after the earthquake in Turkey. Her English was very good because she traveled when she was in school. And her dance troupe traveled in English-speaking countries.

The first time she went to class with Senem, she was surprised and pleased that it was so interesting and fun. "It is like an international party," she told the class. "English classes are very different in Turkey. There the professor is the only one who talks, unless you are in an advanced conversation seminar. They teach with grammar books and exercises. Sometimes it is very boring. We have fun like this only in International Club."

"You can find classes like that in the U.S., too," said Karen. "But it's boring for me also. I like including discussions and lessons on topics the students want to learn more about, like pregnancy and the body and customs about having a baby now that Senem is pregnant. She is so excited that you are here. And I'm happy as well."

"I think I will learn as much as Senem."

Later that afternoon Ruth called. "Hey, Senem. I've been thinking. I want to give you a baby shower."

"But my class is having baby shower next week."

"Oh yeah? Cool. You'll really get a lot of presents. That's great!"

"Is too much, I think. Maybe you can come to the shower of the class."

"Maybe. Hey, why don't you give me Karen's number, and we'll work something out."

❖

Senem felt many emotions—joy, sadness, anger, and confusion—in her long talks with her sister. They cried and laughed as they discussed their family and the changes since the earthquake, the bad and good experiences in America, especially the kidnapping and Emine's death, their hopes and dreams for the future, and Hulya's love life. Senem remembered how Hulya used to advise her about boys. Now Senem felt she had lived a lifetime in the past year. She shared her insight.

"Just listen to your heart and wait until the answer comes to you." Senem thought back to the decision to have another baby, and how it just came to her in a quiet moment.

"You are a wise woman," Hulya told her sister. *"That is the best advice anyone ever gave me."*

❖

By now, in English class they moved into the end-of-the-year projects: reports about countries of the world and a readers' theater play for the kindergarten and first grade classes in the school. No one spoke about the baby shower, but it was still written on the class calendar for May 26.

May 24 was a warm spring day. The fruit trees and iris were in full bloom. Senem, Hasan, and Hulya finished lunch and decided to take a walk. The phone rang just as they were leaving. It was Ruth, wanting to go on a walk, too.

"We will come to your house. Then we can go together to the park," said Senem.

"Great. See you in a minute."

Ruth's door was open, letting fresh air into the house through the screen. They knocked and Ruth called out, "The door's open. Come on in. I'm in the back."

All of a sudden, many voices shouted, "SURPRISE!"

Senem was stunned into silence. She looked around. She saw Karen, Martha, her husband, Carmen, and nearly her whole class. Tarkan and some of their friends from the university were there, too. Hulya burst out in laughter. "It worked! Senem is really surprised."

Ruth said, "You didn't have a clue, did you, Senem? I called Karen and Martha and Hulya. We had such fun planning this."

❖

When the party was over, they needed two cars to get themselves and all the presents back to the apartment. Everyone had been so generous. Hulya had explained to Ruth that they wouldn't have a lot

of room in their baggage allotment when they went back to Turkey. Ruth and Karen planned it so some of the presents were books and toys for Hasan, the big (and possibly jealous) brother. Other presents were for Senem, so she could relax during the hectic first weeks, like bath salts and soothing music CDs. But most were for the new baby: little shirts and shorts, blankets, rattles, books, and stuffed animals, and a car seat and an umbrella stroller.

That night in bed, Senem said to Tarkan, "We have wonderful friends here. I am going to miss them so much. I don't know how I am going to say goodbye."

CHAPTER 10

Early one morning in late June, Senem felt her first labor pains. *"Tarkan, Tarkan, wake up,"* said Senem.

"Time to get up?" mumbled Tarkan.

Senem shook his shoulder. *"I'm having contractions. I timed them. They're every ten minutes."*

Tarkan rolled toward her. He opened his eyes. *"What?"*

"Contractions! The baby's coming! Tarkan, wake up!"

Suddenly, Tarkan rolled the other way. He misjudged the side of the bed and fell on the floor. He landed with a loud thud. All the covers went with him.

Senem sighed. *"Stop being silly. This isn't our first baby."*

"Sorry," said Tarkan from the floor. *"I didn't mean to roll off."* He peeked up over the side of the bed. *"What time is it?"*

"It's about 6 AM."

"Time to get up," muttered Tarkan.

Senem gasped as a contraction hit. She lay on her side, breathing deeply, until it passed. By that time, Tarkan was on the telephone with Ruth. He was wearing blue jeans and his pajama top. Senem wondered whether she should tell him. Then she decided she should be happy he was up and half-dressed. He could worry about proper clothes later.

"*Why are you calling Ruth?*" she asked. "*Hulya is here.*"

Tarkan hung up. "*You're right. Everything is ready. Let's go!*"

"*We have to wake up Hulya, don't we? Why don't you wash your face and get her, and I'll make some tea?*"

"*Tea? That sounds good. Yes, tea. But I'll make it. You wash your face.*"

"*Tarkan, have you lost your mind? I don't want tea, I'll make it for you! My face is—*"

She felt the wave of the next contraction and held her arm out to Tarkan. "*Help me to the sofa!*" she said. "*And wake up Hulya!*"

Tarkan gently took her hand and put his arm around her. He helped her to the couch. He rubbed her back while she breathed through the contraction. He finally seemed to be awake and ready to take charge.

"*Senem, that wasn't ten minutes. I don't think we can wait for Ruth. Let's leave her a note and take Hasan with us.*"

"*Ruth? Tarkan! Wake up Hulya! Right now!*"

Tarkan rushed to Hasan's room and woke up

Hulya. She was noticeably calmer than Tarkan. She took charge.

"Okay, Tarkan, get Senem's bag. It's in the bathroom. I'll take care of Hasan. If you don't stop making so much noise, he's going to wake up. Be quiet!"

Hulya kissed Senem on the cheek and waved them away to the hospital.

At the hospital everything went quickly and smoothly. Senem was in labor for six hours, and then, with a final push, delivered a beautiful seven-pound baby girl. The nurse put the red-faced infant on Senem's chest. She took a deep breath, inhaling the wonderful, earthy, newborn smell of her daughter.

She looked at Tarkan, and he looked at her.

"Say hello to Ruhane," said Senem.

"Hello, sweet Ruhane," said Tarkan quietly.

Ankara, Turkey, September 6

Dear Ruth,

Once upon a time (!) a man told that, "I could die in Istanbul if I didn't see Baku." Now, I'm telling that, "I could die in Ankara if I didn't see Denver."

I have been in Ankara almost for two months and still I don't have my own home and stay in home of my mom. I recognize

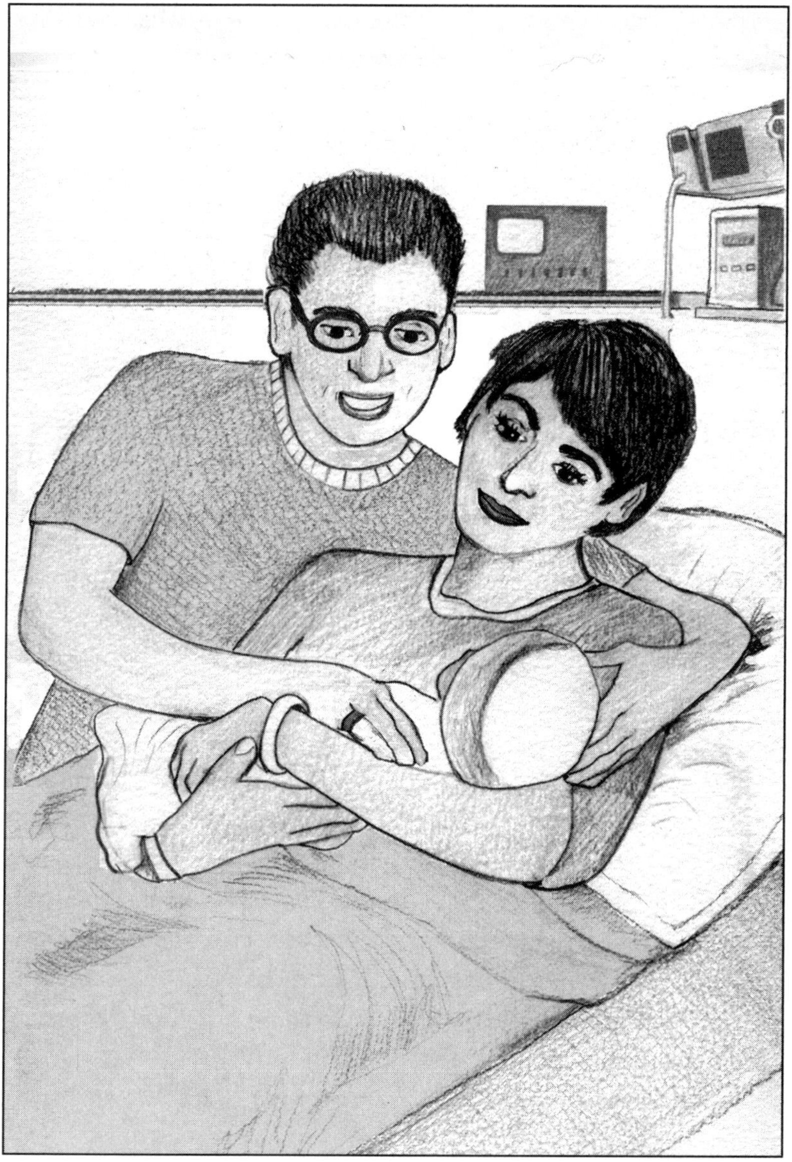

everyday that I forgot the life how hard in Turkey when I was in Denver.

Traffic is terrible. I'm not sure if I can drive in that kind of traffic. There is no rule, everybody drive like the road is their backyard. Every day, when Tarkan and I go to our office I pray that, "Please, I have to live for my children, they need me, maybe twenty years later I can have an accident, but not now!"

Tarkan and I talked, and we think it is better to live in the town. Remember, we talked about buying that house outside of town, but we changed our mind. Everything is far, and Tarkan is traveling for work all the time. He is very busy, and so am I. Now, we are waiting for our new apartment in the town. I hope everything will be better in next ten days.

Hasan and Ruhane are good. When we move our own house, we will send Hasan to school. My mom takes care of Hasan and Ruhane together. Ruhane is so big now. She is 15 pounds. She is happy baby, she smiles, she talks, and she plays with little toys. If you could see each other now, I'm sure you and Ruhane would talk hours and hours.

Ruth, when we left Denver you and Karen and Martha were so kind. You gave us party and presents. I don't say we remember you when we use them because you know that we never forget any of you! I can't forget your friendship, your support when I was sad, and your generosity. You are very brave because you gave your car to an inexperienced driver, like me.

Tell Martha and Karen I will write to them, but I don't know when. I have many friends and a big family, and all want some of my time! Give everyone a big, big, hug for me, and tell them I think of Denver and my wonderful life there often.

Love,

Senem